PERSONAL COUNSELING

Third Edition

Richard L. Knowdell
and
Elwood N. Chapman

A FIFTY MINUTE™ SERIES BOOK

Property Of
Staff Training & Development Program
Return To: Personnel Office,
Humboldt State University,
Student & Business Srvcs. Bldg., Suite 143,
Arcata, CA   95521-8299

CRISP PUBLICATIONS, INC.
Menlo Park, California

PERSONAL COUNSELING
Third Edition

Richard L. Knowdell and Elwood N. Chapman

CREDITS
Editor: **Michael G. Crisp and Gabriella Chapman**
Layout and Composition: **Interface Studio**
Cover Design: **Carol Harris**
Artwork: **Ralph Mapson**

All rights reserved. No part of this book may be reproduced or transmitted in any form or by any means now known or to be invented, electronic or mechanical, including photocopying, recording, or by any information storage or retrieval system without written permission from the author or publisher, except for the brief inclusion of quotations in a review.

Copyright © 1986, 1988, 1993 by Crisp Publications, Inc.
Printed in the United States of America

English language Crisp books are distributed worldwide. Our major international distributors include:

CANADA: Reid Publishing Ltd., Box 69559—109 Thomas St., Oakville, Ontario, Canada L6J 7R4. TEL: (905) 842-4428, FAX: (905) 842-9327

Raincoast Books Distribution Ltd., 112 East 3rd Avenue, Vancouver, British Columbia, Canada V5T 1C8. TEL: (604) 873-6581, FAX: (604) 874-2711

AUSTRALIA: Career Builders, P.O. Box 1051, Springwood, Brisbane, Queensland, Australia 4127. TEL: 841-1061, FAX: 841-1580

NEW ZEALAND: Career Builders, P.O. Box 571, Manurewa, Auckland, New Zealand. TEL: 266-5276, FAX: 266-4152

JAPAN: Phoenix Associates Co., Mizuho Bldg. 2-12-2, Kami Osaki, Shinagawa-Ku, Tokyo 141, Japan. TEL: 3-443-7231, FAX: 3-443-7640

Selected Crisp titles are also available in other languages. Contact International Rights Manager Suzanne Kelly at (415) 323-6100 for more information.

Library of Congress Catalog Card Number 92-054366
Richard L. Knowdell and Elwood N. Chapman
Personal Counseling: Helping Others Help Themselves
ISBN 1-56052-184-8

This book is printed on recyclable paper with soy ink.

PREFACE

Most books on counseling are written for professionals, psychologists, clinicians, or others seeking certification as professional counselors. Yet almost everyone becomes involved in counseling in a more informal sense. Thus most people need to understand and be able to apply basic (nonclinical) techniques of good counseling.

Personal Counseling is designed for the layperson. Although it teaches some of the techniques and principles used by professionals, it was written for managers, supervisors, financial and retirement counselors, law officers, or parents—**anyone who needs to learn good counseling techniques even though they do not have the time to take courses prepared for professionals. It is also ideal for peer counseling.**

This book is designed to be read with a pencil. You will be encouraged to complete a number of exercises that provide an opportunity to apply the concepts presented. Once completed, you can strengthen your counseling skills even further by using the material presented for review and follow-up.

GOOD LUCK!

VOLUNTARY
CONTRACT*

I, _____ , hereby agree to

(Your name)

meet with the individual designated below within thirty days

to discuss my progress toward incorporating the counseling

techniques and ideas presented in this book into my behavioral

patterns. The purpose of this meeting will be to review my

areas of strengths and weaknesses discovered from reading and

applying what I have learned and to list areas where

improvement may still be required.

_____

Signature of individual reading book.

I agree to meet with the above individual on

_____
Month   *Date*   *Time*

at the following location.

_____

_____
Signature of individual (manager, mentor, etc.) reviewing my progress.

*The purpose of this agreement is to motivate you to
incorporate important concepts and techniques into your daily
activities. It also provides a degree of accountability between
you and the person you select to sign the agreement.

ABOUT THIS BOOK

PERSONAL COUNSELING: HELPING OTHERS HELP THEMSELVES is not like most books. It has a unique ''self-paced'' format that encourages a reader to become personally involved. Designed to be ''read with a pencil,'' there are an abundance of exercises, activities, assessments and cases that invite participation.

The objective of *PERSONAL COUNSELING* is to help a person develop the basic techniques that make for an effective and successful counselor.

PERSONAL COUNSELING (and the other self-improvement books listed in the back of this book) can be used effectively in a number of ways. Here are some possibilities:

- Individual Study. Because the book is self-instructional, all that is needed is a quiet place, some time and a pencil. Completing the activities and exercises, should provide not only valuable feedback, but also practical ideas about steps for self-improvement.

- Workshops and Seminars. This book is ideal for pre-assigned reading prior to a workshop or seminar. With the basics in hand, the quality of participation should improve. More time can be spent on concept extensions and applications during the program. The book is also effective when distributed at the beginning of a session.

- Remote Location Training. Copies can be sent to those not able to attend ''home office'' training sessions.

- Informal Study Groups. Thanks to the format, brevity and low cost, this book is ideal for ''brown-bag'' or other informal group sessions.

There are other possibilities that depend on the objectives of the user. One thing for sure, even after it has been read, this book will serve as excellent reference material which can be easily reviewed. Good luck!

CONTENTS

(Continued on next page)

CONTENTS (Continued)

P A R T

I

You Have The
Right Stuff

4

> "I have found that the best way to give advice to your children is to find out what they want and then advise them to do it."
>
> Harry S. Truman

COUNSELING IS A PROVEN WAY TO HELP
OTHERS SORT OUT AND SOLVE PROBLEMS.
COUNSELING IS USUALLY ACCOMPLISHED
PRIVATELY ON A ONE-ON-ONE BASIS. THERE
IS NO MAGIC TO THE TECHNIQUES, METHODS,
AND PRINCIPLES OF COUNSELING. THEY
CAN BE LEARNED AND APPLIED BY ANYONE.

MAKE YOUR CHOICE NOW

SUCCESSFUL COUNSELORS	FAILURES
Use accepted techniques	Don't use accepted techniques
Let the person being counseled do most of the talking	Do most of the talking themselves
Listen to *all* the person being counseled has to say	Listen only superficially and then jump to conclusions
Make appropriate suggestions in a sensitive way	Criticize
Paraphrase or repeat back what they *think* the other person said	Inject their own interpretations
Stay cool and collected	Let their emotions get away from them
Honor the rule of confidentiality	Don't honor the rule of confidentiality
Acknowledge the other person's *values* and provide the guidance based on *those* values	Impose *their* values on the person being counseled
View counseling as an orderly process with certain rules	Make up their rules as they go
Provide the guidance needed to assist a person to make his or her own decision	Make decisions for the person being counseled
Provide support and reinforcement after a decision has been made	End interviews abruptly and move on to something else

Add your own:

_____   _____

_____   _____

_____   _____

OPPORTUNITIES

HUMAN CONFLICTS

Everyone has had conflicts involving other people. There is no escape. Althought not all human conflicts can be resolved, counseling usually offers the best hope. Someone, however, must **initiate** the private discussion. If you are a supervisor and one of your employees has become a problem, you are the one who should intervene and see if the problem can be solved through counseling. If you have a problem with a friend over whom you have no authority, you can **still** initiate a communication session (counseling) that may help resolve things. Once you learn basic counseling skills–and learn how to use them–you will develop more confidence. All of this should help reduce the amount of human conflict in *your* life.

WHERE COUNSELING SKILLS CAN BE PUT TO USE

Most of us are surrounded with opportunities to become counselors. Learning to recognize and become involved in those we encounter can enhance our careers and personal lives. Place a check in those areas that provide you with opportunities for counseling.

☐ **AS A MANAGER OF EMPLOYEES:** Counseling is recognized as a vital management tool and most supervisors use counseling almost daily.

☐ **AS A YOUTH LEADER:** A scout leader or athletic coach who is responsible for the behavior of others needs some basic counseling skills.

☐ **AS AN ADVISOR IN A BUSINESS SITUATION:** A banker, insurance agent, or financial counselor is often the first ''outsider'' to assist a client facing a problem.

☐ **AS A PARENT:** It is usually more difficult for a parent to counsel a son or daughter than other outsiders.

☐ **AS A FRIEND:** Sometimes, through sensitive counseling, we are in a position to help a close friend solve a problem.

☐ **AS A TEACHER (SCHOOL OR CHURCH):** Many teachers are involved with informal counseling of their students.

☐ **AS A MILITARY LEADER:** Commissioned and noncommissioned military officers often need counseling skills to perform the people part of their responsibilities.

☐ **AS A PEER COUNSELOR:** High schools, colleges and other youth organizations have discovered that outstanding students and leaders make superior counselors with peers when adequately trained.

☐ **AS A SOCIAL WORKER:** Although their time is often limited, social workers and probation officers need a high level of counseling skills to perform their roles.

☐ **AS A PLACEMENT PERSON:** Career guidance and placement officers are primarily personal counselors because most clients need to overcome barriers in seeking new jobs.

☐ **AS A RETIREMENT PLANNER:** Counseling is a primary tool for those seeking to help others make the transition to retirement and make the most of their later years.

OCCASIONALLY ALL ADULTS DISCOVER THEMSELVES IN THE ROLE OF A PERSONAL COUNSELOR—ONLY A FEW ARE PREPARED.

THE RANGE OF COUNSELING SITUATIONS

Throughout this book, counseling situations will be frequently addressed as ''problems'' that can best be resolved by two people—the person with the problem and the individual with the counseling skills. The counselor, in effect, is in the role of the advisor.

Not all situations where a counselor can be used to advantage involve problems. At times, making a choice between two opportunities is involved, as in the case of helping a student select the best college to attend. Sometimes it is a crossroad situation where the individual being counseled needs some backup guidance as to which road to take. At other times a problem has been solved, the direction determined, and all that is needed by the counselee is some reinforcement. When a counselor starts out to help another person, she or he may not know what kind of support might be needed.

Counseling situations fall into many categories.

Relationships. The largest category involves relationship conflicts. Some are work related, others are family oriented. A sensitive and discreet personal counselor can usually play a significant role in resolving such conflicts. On occasion, however, they should be referred to a professional.

Lifestyle. People often need help in knowing how to live their lives. Where should they live? Do they need a religious affiliation? What about life goals? Careers? Retirement? Financial guidance? Often it is best to see a financial advisor, a career guidance specialist, or someone who counsels people on retirement options. Most personal counselors can be helpful with lifestyle problems or they can make referrals to specialists.

Personal. Although nonprofessional personal counselors can play an important role in helping others develop self-esteem, build stronger self-images, and restore positive attitudes, they can go only so far before they need to make a referral to a licensed counselor or psychologist. Deep-seated mental and emotional problems must always be turned over to professionals who are trained and licensed to provide therapy.

Miscellaneous. There are other areas where the personal counselor is not expected to have expertise and is therefore disqualified. Legal and tax problems are examples, as are medical problems, including chemical dependency.

Personal counselors make their best contribution in helping others solve problems that they are capable of solving themselves, but need guidance and support from another person to do so.

Case studies help provide insights you may not already possess. Seven case problems are included in this program. Please give each your careful attention.

The case on the opposite page will help you understand some items involved in becoming a successful counselor.

CASE 1

WHO WILL MAKE THE BEST COUNSELOR?

Byron and Ginger are new supervisors for a large service organization. On Friday both will attend a company-sponsored seminar designed to teach effective counseling skills to deal with problem employees and enhance productivity. Byron views the day as an opportunity to contribute; Ginger has some misgivings.

Byron has already demonstrated good management skills. He is excellent at delegating, setting priorities, making decisions and communicating—especially in group situations. Byron is a high-tempo supervisor who knows how to build strong relationships with superiors. It is also obvious that Byron cares for people, especially his own employees. In his younger days, he spent several summers as a camp counselor. Although a business administration major at the university, his early interest in people caused him to minor in psychology.

Ginger is as qualified as Byron academically (she was an accounting major with a minor in data processing), however her future appears more limited. Where Byron likes to be out front, Ginger prefers to stay in the background and let her accomplishments speak for themselves. Ginger is not as good at group communication and is content to participate in less-obvious ways. She is not looking forward to Friday because she feels the word "counselor" implies someone who uses psychological techniques to manipulate others. Ginger is an outstanding listener who is extremely patient with her employees; however, she does not view herself as a counselor. She wants to build a strong, efficient staff, but feels uncomfortable giving advice, especially when it is of a personal nature. During her first formal appraisal Ginger's superior wrote on the rating form: "Outstanding learner."

Grade Byron and Ginger on how skillful you believe they will be in using basic counseling skills. Assign a letter grade of A, B, C, D, or F.

SKILL	BYRON	GINGER
Creating a comfortable counseling atmosphere	_____	_____
Being objective	_____	_____
Using tested techniques	_____	_____
Keeping communications confidential	_____	_____
Being sensitive in giving advice	_____	_____
Being patient	_____	_____
Providing follow-up support	_____	_____

Who do you think will become the better counselor? Turn to page 92 for the view of the authors.

COUNSELING IS A
COMMUNICATIONS CHALLENGE!

Unfortunately, the term "counselor" is often misinterpreted. Some think only of authority figures such as lawyers and psychiatrists. Others believe a person can become a counselor only after formal graduate training and a license.

In reality, a counselor is an advisor and interviewer who communicates on a one-on-one basis. A counselor can talk seriously with another person about a problem or situation.

Chances are good you are **already** involved in counseling. In approximately fifty minutes, you should be better prepared to counsel others.

WHAT CAN BECOMING A GOOD COUNSELOR OR ADVISOR DO FOR YOU?

People underestimate the advantages in learning how to become a skillful one-to-one communicator. More than you may think, developing this skill could be your *key* to a better future. Place a check in the square opposite those statements that are important to you.

☐   1.   Becoming a better counselor can help improve my career opportunities...especially it I get into management.

☐   2.   Learning to counsel others will add to my personal confidence.

☐   3.   Learning to work with others on a one-on-one basis will improve my communication skills.

☐   4.   Helping others will give me more personal satisfaction and self-respect.

☐   5.   Becoming a better advisor will help me build better, more rewarding relationships.

☐   6.   Improving counseling skills will help me become a better parent and/or leader.

☐   7.   Learning to counsel will help me recognize and solve my own problems.

☐   8.   Helping others will make me feel I am making a contribution.

☐   9.   Working as a counselor will help me improve critical listening skills.

☐   10.   Counseling others will help me better understand myself.

YOU DO NOT NEED TO BE AN EXTROVERT TO BE A SUCCESSFUL COUNSELOR. QUIET, THOUGHTFUL PEOPLE OFTEN ARE MORE SUCCESSFUL.

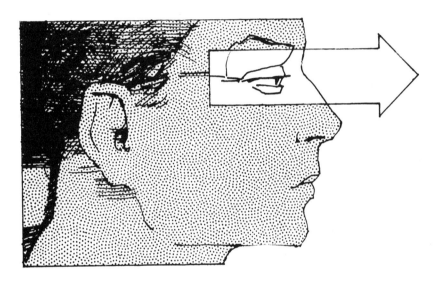

PRE-TEST

RATING YOUR COUNSELING SKILLS

This exercise is designed to measure your basic counseling skills. At this stage don't worry if you have a less-than-perfect score. After you have had an opportunity to practice the counseling skills covered in this book, you will be able to measure your progress by taking this exercise again.

Read each statement and then circle the number you feel best fits you.

A lower number (1 or 2) indicates you are weak in the area. A high number (4 or 5) indicates strength.

		Weak			Strong	
1.	I need to practice a newly learned skill before I use it for real.	1	2	3	4	5
2.	I can accept others as worthy individuals even if I don't like aspects of their behavior.	1	2	3	4	5
3.	I can wait until I hear all a person has to say before I form an opinion and decide on a response.	1	2	3	4	5
4.	When appropriate, I will paraphrase what a person has said to confirm that I heard them accurately.	1	2	3	4	5
5.	I am generally optimistic and look for possible solutions rather than roadblocks.	1	2	3	4	5
6.	I try to understand behavior objectively before branding it as ''appropriate'' or ''inappropriate.''	1	2	3	4	5
7.	People who know me trust me to keep a confidence.	1	2	3	4	5
8.	I try to help friends make their own decisions, rather than ask them to accept what I think is the best solution.	1	2	3	4	5
9.	I am someone people feel they can turn to in troubled times for support.	1	2	3	4	5
10.	I would feel comfortable helping others even if they were older and more experienced than myself.	1	2	3	4	5

SCORING: If you scored under thirty-five, you will most likely benefit from learning and applying the counseling skills presented in this book.

You probably already have some of the personality traits that help make a successful counselor.

PERSONAL TRAITS OF SUCCESSFUL COUNSELORS

Below are 10 personality traits found in successful counselors. Place a plus in the square opposite those you already possess; a minus mark opposite those you feel can be better developed in the future; and a question mark in any remaining squares.

☐ Patient

☐ Perceptive and sensitive

☐ Likes people

☐ Nonthreatening demeanor

☐ Sense of humor

☐ Desire to help

☐ Positive attitude

☐ Good listener

☐ Warm personality

☐ Problem solver

With time and patience, almost everyone can learn to be comfortable and effective as a counselor. For example, in case 2 you will be introduced to three people who have vastly different personalities, yet each can learn to be an excellent counselor. Of course, one may have characteristics that make it easier, but all have *enough* of the right stuff to become effective. As you make your recommendations in this case, please keep in mind that it is only the counselee who really knows how effective the counselor has been. And the counselee may not know for years to come.

CASE 2

WHAT CONSTITUTES AN EXCELLENT COUNSELOR?

We all may have in our minds what we would consider to be the ideal or model counselor. Our image may come from our early experiences in school. What we may not realize is that each person has a different image. As you read the short sketches of the following three individuals, try to determine which one would, in your opinion, be the best counselor for *all individuals.*

Geraldine is a no-nonsense person. Her focused concentration allows Geraldine to get to the heart of a matter in a hurry. She is the kind of person who likes to be organized and follow a pattern. Some of her co-workers say she is overstructured and insensitive. Her superiors consider her to be highly productive and professional. Would Geraldine find it easy to become a counselor?

Jack is a people person. Whenever a problem arises in his department, he thinks of the people under his supervision first and technical matters second. He is the kind of person that you might enjoy as a teacher or clergyman. Many co-workers claim Jack is a compassionate person with great patience. His superiors consider him to be a time-waster who overidentifies with people while departmental productivity suffers. Would you consider Jack to be a "natural" as a counselor?

Genevieve is popular among all ages and cultures. Her popularity stems from her good nature. Genevieve loves to tell jokes and always seems to see the funny side of any situation. Her co-workers miss her when she is absent. Her superiors consider Genevieve to be flighty and frivolous. When she settles down she can be most effective, but it is doubtful her boss would recommend her to be a supervisor. Would you like to have Genevieve as a counselor?

If you could select one single characteristic or behavioral trait from each of the three individuals that would help them become *effective* counselors, what would it be?

Geraldine _____

Jack _____

Genevieve _____

Which of the three would you say has the greatest *potential* to become an excellent personal counselor? Why? See page 92 for views of the Authors.

THE ESSENCE OF COUNSELING

Counseling is communication. It is talking things over. It is searching for a solution. Because counseling deals with feelings it is a sensitive process. Although counseling does not always work, in many situations it offers the best hope for a solution. Even when a solution is not forthcoming, those involved may be able to live with the situation with more grace. There is little to lose.

Yet despite the hope counseling offers, many hesitate to use the approach. Knowing *why* you avoid the process can help you initiate it more often and improve not only your career but also your life.

On the following page are some common excuses people use for not making the most of counseling.

WHY PEOPLE DELAY

Please place a check mark in those squares opposite reasons why you might hesitate to use counseling as a technique.

☐ Let sleeping dogs lie.

☐ Time will solve the problem.

☐ I can't keep my emotions out of the process.

☐ I'm afraid I'll open up a can of worms.

☐ I might say the wrong thing.

☐ Getting things started bothers me.

☐ I have little faith in counseling.

☐ I'm uncomfortable in the role of a counselor.

☐ Others may laugh at my amateurish approach.

☐ I'm not good at communicating.

☐ I don't like arguments.

☐ The risk is greater than the reward.

☐ There is too much involved to do it right.

☐ It is just not my thing.

☐ I'm afraid I'll get in too deep.

☐ It takes too much time.

IF AT ANY TIME YOU SENSE YOU ARE OVER YOUR HEAD TRYING TO HELP OTHERS SOLVE A PROBLEM, SAY SO AND THEN HELP THEM MAKE A CONNECTION WITH A LICENSED PROFESSIONAL. SOME INDIVIDUALS MAY HAVE PROBLEMS YOU ARE NOT PREPARED TO DEAL WITH.

COUNSELING STYLE

When you assume the role of a counselor, picture yourself in a private, comfortable room discussing a problem with a friend. Be comfortable and relaxed.

It is vital for you to feel good about your personality and style. Be yourself. If you try to be somebody else (a lawyer or psychologist), it will probably be awkward and you will communicate poorly.

TIPS AHEAD

THE PSYCHOLOGY OF COUNSELING

Here are some tips to help you learn ways to become a good counselor.

Be a Guide, Not the Leader—Your role is to guide others to decisions that will be best for *them*. You don't make the decision, they do. Although two heads are often better than one, your head should play a minor role.

Be Someone Who Helps Another Resolve a Problem—A problem burdens the other party, not you. When you help a person solve that problem, you lighten the burden they carry. It is a win-win situation. They feel better, and you feel rewarded about the role you played in the process.

Promote Self-Esteem—You may need to instill some self-confidence and build self-esteem in the other party before they can sort out and solve their problems. When you listen respectfully and say the right things at the right time, you make others more capable. Sometimes this is the key for a good solution.

Be a Person Who Takes the Initiative—Intervention counseling is difficult. When another party seeks you out for advice, everything is in your favor. The "climate" is usually positive. However, when you must intervene because a person's problem is causing distress (or lower productivity) among others, you have a more difficult challenge. When you are successful with intervention counseling everyone comes out ahead.

Foster Independence, Not Dependence—Counseling assumes a different dimension when you attempt to help a party you supervise or live with. In such cases it is a good idea to keep the **Mutual Reward Theory** in mind. The idea is to make sure you and the other party receive rewards from each other and that the reward system is understood. Identifying such rewards during a counseling session can be productive. Once identified—and the rewards are earned—a relationship is strengthened and further counseling may not be necessary.

Be Comfortable to Know—The idea behind all counseling is to help others understand their problems, seek solutions, and take action.

Be Honest About Your Role—Tell the person being counseled what you can and cannot do. Communicate that your job is to guide them to a solution of their own—nothing more.

Transmit Confidence—Leave people confident that they can solve their own problems and improve their lives.

''He who can take advice is sometimes superior to him who can give it.''

Karl von Knebel (1744-1834)

II

Setting The Stage

The Five Rs
Of Counseling

GETTING IT *RIGHT*!

Personal counseling occurs when two people have the opportunity to sit down and quietly talk things over. It is a private conversation that leads one party to the solution of a problem. Normally, those being counseled enter the session with a heavy load on their shoulders and, at the end, walk away knowing their load is lighter.

A counseling session can be a rich experience for both parties. The person being counseled can find a solution to a problem, make a difficult decision, and feel much better about life. The counselor can have that warm feeling of satisfaction that comes from knowing that another person can now cope better.

But a productive and helpful meeting does not occur automatically. Rather, it must be designed and implemented by the counselor. First, the atmosphere or climate for good communications must be present. Next, a predetermined process must be followed to isolate and resolve the problem. Toward the end, the person being counseled must accept or ''own'' the solution and reestablish his or her goals.

Sound complicated?

At the beginning, yes. But once you master the techniques involved, it will all come together and, with experience, you will become skillful and effective.

To get off on the right foot, you must first become acquainted with and practice the Five Rs of counseling:

- Right purpose
- Right time
- Right place
- Right approach
- Right techniques

THE FIVE Rs

THE RIGHT PURPOSE

Counseling—talking things over—is a way to solve problems that have not or will not solve themselves in other ways. Sometimes the counselor (supervisor, parent, clergy, friend, youth leader) will encourage a meeting, at other times the individual will bring a problem to the counselor. Whenever two people can talk over a problem and seek the best answer, the purpose is usually right. There are, however, some exceptions.

THE PURPOSE IS RIGHT

- When a work problem has surfaced
- What there is a family misunderstanding
- When something personal is involved

THE PURPOSE IS WRONG

- When the counselor wants to play psychologist
- When the counselor wants to exploit or manipulate the person being counseled
- When the counselor uses the situation to probe too deeply into the affairs of the person being counseled

GOOD PURPOSE

Helen came to Ruth, a close friend, to help her work through a problem she was having with her ex-husband. Ruth listened carefully to Helen's point of view. Finally they isolated the problem and came up with two potential solutions. At this point, Ruth asked if she could make an appointment for Helen with a professional family counselor to make sure they were on the right track. Helen agreed and Ruth offered to go with her if that was her desire.

WRONG PURPOSE

When Sara developed a serious conflict with her supervisor, she took the problem to her boyfriend Frank. Frank was pleased because it gave him an opportunity to get to know Sara better and make her more dependent upon him. Frank wanted to help her resolve the conflict but he also had ulterior motives. His purpose was not 100 percent to help Sara in an objective manner, so his purpose was wrong.

To consider yourself a counselor, your purpose must be to assist the person being counseled to solve his or her problem. *Nothing else.*

THE RIGHT TIME

To have a successful counseling session, both parties need to be relaxed and comfortable so that communication is free and easy. It is most difficult to select a time that is ideal and pressure-free for both parties. When the chips are down, the counselor should make the major adjustment. In other words, select the best time for the person being counseled because nothing will go right when the person who has the problem is on edge because the timing is wrong.

Selecting the right time is, in part, the problem before the problem. What is right for one person may be a pressure point for another. Take your own circumstances as an example. On a typical day, when would be the best time for you to work with a counselor? Place a check opposite the three times of day best for you.

- ☐ A breakfast meeting

- ☐ Before lunch in an office

- ☐ Just before leaving work

- ☐ Late at night

- ☐ At lunch

- ☐ At dinner

- ☐ Over cocktails before dinner

- ☐ On a day off

- ☐ While driving home

- ☐ On a pleasure trip

Under which time situation would you be least threatened? Which time would fit best into your schedule if you wanted a meeting tomorrow? Would you accept any time that the counselor had free?

At first, it may sound like one time is almost as good as another, but for maximum results timing is most important. In cases where two people are seeking help from the same counselor, timing can be critical.

In addition to the right time, *enough time* is vital. Generally speaking, a minimum of 40 minutes is needed for one counseling session.

THE RIGHT PLACE

Selecting the least threatening location for the person to be counseled is critical. Selecting a spot where you, as the counselor, can be comfortable is equally important. The five criteria to use in choosing the best possible location are:

1. There must be peace and quiet, a place where communication can be private and confidential.

2. The location should be isolated so there are few, if any, observers.

3. The atmosphere should be informal and nonthreatening. The counselor and counselee should be able to communicate on an equal basis.

4. If a telephone is present, it should be disconnected or a switchboard operator should not put through calls.

5. Where possible, the setting should be as close to nature as possible. If an office must be used, it should have a pleasant, outdoor decor without a desk between the counselor and counselee.

Based upon the above criteria, which of the following locations would you prefer if you were the counselee? Please place a checkmark opposite your three preferences.

☐ Park bench   ☐ While taking a walk

☐ Restaurant booth   ☐ While riding in a car

☐ Closed office   ☐ Picnic table

☐ On an airplane   ☐ At the beach

☐ Living room   ☐ Other: _____

In some cases, taking a short trip to a different and relaxing environment is helpful. This is especially true in highly charged family situations. Most of the time it is best to let the person with the problem choose the location. As a personal counselor, the motto "have patience, will travel" is a good one. Professional counselors have the luxury of remaining in their offices.

THE RIGHT APPROACH

Counseling meetings usually get started in one of two ways. First is when someone who has a problem comes to you. Second is when you must intervene and set up the meeting yourself.

VOLUNTARY MEETINGS. When someone respects you enough that they will come to you and say, ''Will you help me work through a problem?'' everything is going your way. Barriers are down. The counselee *wants* to listen. Even under these ideal conditions it remains possible to make some major mistakes. Here are two to avoid.

1. Just because the person needing help comes to you on a voluntary basis doesn't mean he or she is not nervous. The individual may have had a sleepless night getting up enough nerve to approach you. Take time to see that the counselee feels comfortable with you and the environment chosen before you initiate the process.

2. Because the individual has come to you over other people, you may interpret this to mean that you can overtalk and unload more advice than you should. *Avoid this at all costs.*

INTERVENTION COUNSELING. This is when you sense a problem that is hurting others or yourself and you step in as a counselor to assist. There are two ways to do this. First, you can use the oblique approach. This is when you move in quietly with an indirect or ''soft'' approach. For example, you might use the following invitations:

''Let's do lunch tomorrow and have a chat.'' ''Can you drop by my office for an overdue discussion on a matter of importance to both of us?''

The oblique approach may be best when you suspect a misunderstanding and want to nip a possible problem in the bud. In short, it is a polite way to set up a counseling session you believe is needed.

The second approach is more direct. You move in quickly and openly because the behavior of the individual may be hurting you or your operation. This may be the best way to get a counseling session under way when a conflict exists between two people—either two people close to you or in your department or another person and you. For example, you might use these more forceful and direct invitations.

''We need to talk.'' ''Can you give me an hour of your time this afternoon? We have something to resolve.''

Intervention counseling is difficult to set up, yet once arrangements have been made, the same principles and techniques used in voluntary counseling are applicable. The fact that the situation may be more volatile and emotionally charged does not alter the process that stands the best chance of succeeding.

THE RIGHT TECHNIQUES

When it comes to counseling, techniques are useful but simple ways of helping others reach elegant solutions to their problems or opportunities. Techniques are tools to facilitate communication.

Dozens of techniques make up the counseling process. Some will fit into your personal comfort zone. Others will not. When you have discovered and woven certain techniques into your behavior, you will have created your counseling style. It is the purpose of this book to assist you in doing this.

Your counseling style will include everything from the tone of your voice to the process you follow—how you start, how you end, and how you lead the counselee to his or her solution. Whether your style becomes effective may not be measurable because a counselor can seldom get long-term feedback on the final results of the communication that took place.

View the pages ahead as an introduction to many principles and techniques which, once integrated into your style, will give you a reputation as an excellent personal counselor. Later, should you desire, you can investigate more formal programs leading toward the role of a professional counselor.

THREE WAYS TO BUILD RAPPORT AND, AT THE SAME TIME, GET THE INFORMATION YOU NEED TO HELP THE COUNSELEE MAKE A WISE DECISION

POSITIVE FEEDBACK

Feedback is the *response* you give to what you hear from the person being counseled. It is your reply. There are three forms of positive response.

1. Comfortable silence. A verbal response is not always necessary or advisable. Sometimes a reply to what the individual is saying is an interruption to their train of thought. If given more time, the individual will lead you to the crux of the matter. When you communicate nonverbally that you are comfortable with what is being said you will probably hear more without asking. Although extended silence could be counterproductive, short silences with a smile (when appropriate) can be more encouraging and supportive than words.

After talking his problem over with his coach, Rick felt great about his role in the coming game. Thinking back, Rick realized that he had done 95 percent of the talking and found his own solution. More often than not the coach let silence do his talking.

2. Reinforcement. When people with a problem receive support of any kind from a counselor they usually keep talking and get to the heart of the matter quickly. Examples of verbal support are:

''You are doing a good job of giving me a clear picture of what is bothering you.''

''So far, you have acted in a normal, healthy fashion. I am proud of you.''

''You have done such a good job of giving me the whole story that I think we can work out a solution in the next ten minutes.''

3. Advise. You have heard the expression that the hardest thing in the world to give away is advice. It's true. Most counselors prefer to let the person they are trying to help figure things out on their own with the help of two-way communications. Sometimes, however, people are receptive to advice. In fact, they feel let down if they don't receive some. The following questions can help you discover if the door is open wide enough to risk giving advice.

''Would you like for me to make a suggestion?''

''Are you open to a word of caution?''

''May I offer two possibilities that might solve your problem? Then you can make the choice?''

Using silence in a sensitive way, providing reinforcement effectively, and checking to see if a suggestion may be acceptable are counseling techniques. Use them when they fall into your comfort zone.

IF YOU CRITICIZE
THE PERSON BEING
COUNSELED, YOU TAKE
STEPS BACKWARD.
FIND OUT WHY ON THE
NEXT PAGE.

AVOIDING THE TEMPTATION

Receiving advice can be a positive experience but being on the receiving end of criticism can often do more harm than good. Most effective counselors avoid criticism of any kind for the following reasons:

- Those with little self-esteem find it difficult to receive criticism (it pushes them closer to negative feelings) even though they admit that the criticism was earned and meant to be constructive.

- Criticism generates excuses and often results in the blaming of others.

- Criticism tends to center on one isolated behavior instead of a series of related incidents.

- Criticism decreases the confidence individuals have in themselves.

- Criticism often leads to escape from a problem instead of a possible solution.

- Criticism damages the relationship between counselor and counselee.

- Criticism can cause defensiveness and denial.

Criticism looks back to mistakes of the past that people have already identified. They know they screwed things up. Often they know why. Hearing about it again and devoting more mind-time to the resulting damage does not lead to a solution. What is needed is a positive solution that will make the future brighter.

> After being grounded again for staying out late, Gregg decided that his own high-risk behavior was not getting him anywhere. In a long talk with his father, where he admitted past mistakes, he said he was making changes and hoped he could earn the right to use a family car when he received his license in a few weeks. Instead of dealing with the past, Gregg's father chose a few behavioral areas where positive reinforcement was possible and stated that when Gregg was ready a car would be available for certain occasions.

It is easy, especially for parents, to go back and criticize past behavior by presenting specific examples. When the awareness of past behavior is uppermost in the mind of the person being counseled, switching to the reinforcement technique is refreshing for both parties and can lead to a more positive future.*

---

* For additional information on the dangers of criticizing, see *Coaching & Counseling* by Marianne Minor, Crisp Publications.

INTERVENTION COUNSELING

Waiting for time to solve a problem is a luxury one cannot always afford. This is especially true in the workplace where productivity standards must be achieved. It is equally true in personal situations where the behavior of one individual is destructive to another. Under such circumstances, a meeting needs to be initiated. This is called intervention counseling and often puts counseling skills to a demanding test.

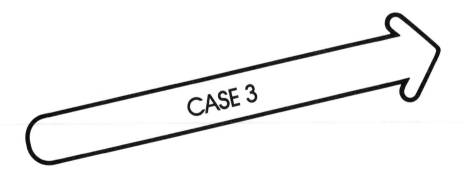

CASE 3

WHICH APPROACH IS BEST?

Justine is increasingly upset over Sally's on-the-job behavior. Employed six weeks ago (at Justine's suggestion) Sally is not living up to her potential. The primary problem seems to be Sally's inability to separate her responsibilities at work from her personal problems. She has been late and absent more than any other member of the staff and she receives far too many phone calls from her children. What makes the situation even more irritating to Justine is the fact that this problem was anticipated and discussed during the employment interview. Sally said: "You need not worry about my home problems. Things are under control."

Justine has asked Sally to join her in her office in ten minutes. She is contemplating which of the following approaches to take.

Approach #1: Use a directive technique. During the first few minutes reflect on the conversation that took place during the interview and then list items that have been taking place. Once this has been done, then ask the question: "What are you going to do about it?"

Approach #2: Use a nondirective technique. Sit back, say very little, and ask Sally how things are going. Do not mention the home situation unless it comes from her. Do not mention that being late and absent is causing problems unless Sally wants to talk about it. Sally will probably feel uncomfortable and do 90 percent of the talking.

Approach #3: Employ the "I'm disappointed" strategy. Say in a nonthreatening way that things are not working out and you thought it best to discuss it. The idea behind this approach is to discover how intense the home problem may be so a solution might be fashioned.

Select the approach that you feel will best lead to a solution to the problem.

I vote for Approach #1 ☐; Approach #2 ☐; Approach #3 ☐ .

See page 92 for views of the Authors.

"If you can tell the difference between good
and bad advice, you don't need advice."

Laurence J. Peter

P A R T

III

Seeking Solutions

The
Counseling
Process

COUNSELING CAN BE COMPARED TO PLAYING BASEBALL

Once the stage has been set and the Five Rs of counseling have been satisfied, the actual process starts. This process—a method of reaching the best results by taking prescribed and successive steps— will give those being counseled the framework by which they will discover the solution to their problem or dilemma.

To simplify this process—and make it more exciting—we are going to compare it with playing baseball. You need not actually play baseball for this comparison or analogy to work but the more you get into the ''game'' the more you will learn and the sooner you will be effective as a personal counselor.

On the following page you will see an illustration of a baseball diamond. The counseling process consists of you guiding or taking the counselee around the bases. The process is not over until the counselee reaches home base and the game has been won (decision made).

As you contemplate going around the bases, keep these baseball terms in mind.

- You can't win them all. Sometimes you may do everything right and the results are disappointing.

- You can't get home without covering all bases. If you get stuck on first, second, or third the process hasn't fulfilled its potential.

- Sometimes—like hitting a home run—you can get around the bases quickly; at other times it can take two or three sessions.

- Every counseling session is a new ballgame because every counselee and every problem is different. That is why you must become a superb listener.

- Think of personal counseling as a game in which you are rooting for the counselee to win.

- If you wish, you can consider yourself the coach.

Please study the baseball diamond before you continue.

IN SUCCESSFUL COUNSELING YOU COVER THE BASES

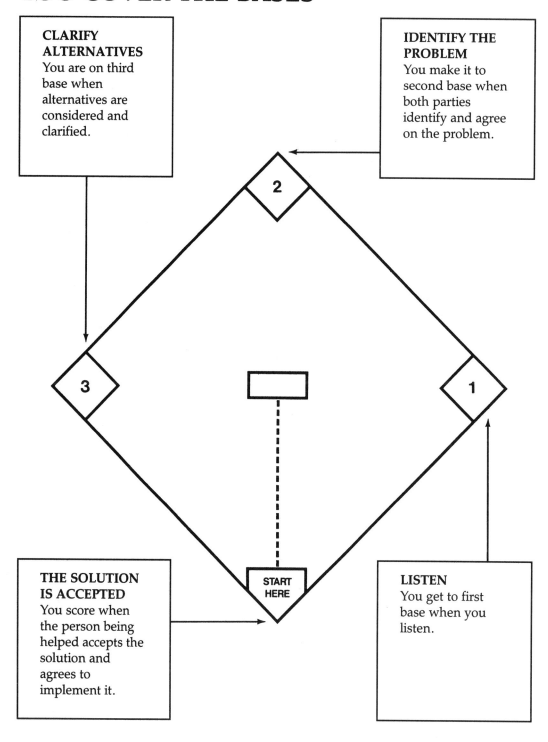

CLARIFY ALTERNATIVES
You are on third base when alternatives are considered and clarified.

IDENTIFY THE PROBLEM
You make it to second base when both parties identify and agree on the problem.

THE SOLUTION IS ACCEPTED
You score when the person being helped accepts the solution and agrees to implement it.

LISTEN
You get to first base when you listen.

START HERE

3

2

1

GIVING ADVANCE NOTICE ABOUT HOW THE COUNSELING GAME IS PLAYED CAN RELAX THE "PLAYER" AND IMPROVE THE PROCESS. SEE THE NEXT PAGE ON HOW TO DO THIS.

$\Rightarrow$

EXPLAINING WHAT LIES AHEAD
(Rules of the Game)

Sometimes, before moving into a counseling session, it may be smart on your part to explain to the counselee the process you will be going through together. Field testing indicates that using the baseball analogy to do this can be most helpful. In other words, show and tell the counselee that both of you will go around the bases step by step and when home plate is reached, the session or sessions will be over. This may relieve some of the apprehension within the counselee about what will happen and enhance the process at the same time. It will also communicate that you are present to guide the individual around the bases. He or she is the player. Not you.

Here is one way you might explain each of the four bases to be covered.

> **First base** is what we are doing now. Getting acquainted, relaxing, accepting each other and preparing to tackle a problem.
>
> **Second base** is viewing the problem from different perspectives so we can be more objective and understand the dimensions of what we are trying to accomplish.
>
> **Third base** is looking at the alternatives so we can weigh and decide which road to take. Two heads can be better than one, but all I can do is make suggestions. In the end, you make the decision.
>
> **Home base** is when you realize you have won the ballgame. You'll feel great when you get there. Shall we start?

In giving the counselee a preview of what is going to happen (your choice), it is important to communicate that the process may require 40 minutes or more, that the counselee must do the real work and that it is important not to get stuck on first, second, or third base.

TIP ON HOW TO GET TO FIRST BASE: MAKE YOUR APPROACH QUIET, FRIENDLY, PERCEPTIVE AND POSITIVE.

HEAD FOR FIRST

FIRST BASE: THE SKILL OF LISTENING

Achieving rapport with the other party will get you to first base. Following are nine tips to help you get there.

The NINE Steps to First Base

1. Send friendly nonverbal signals

2. Give a warm and sincere greeting

3. Demonstrate an immediate desire to help

4. Listen to what is being said

5. Listen to what is *not* being said

6. Listen to what "can't" be said

7. Don't make a judgment too quickly

8. Listen with your ears, eyes *and* your body

9. Ask quality questions to better learn the situation

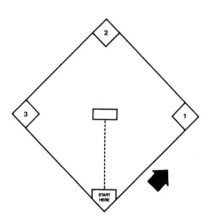

> **THE LESS TALKING YOU DO AS A COUNSELOR,
> THE MORE EFFECTIVE YOU WILL BE**

TO REACH SECOND BASE
IT IS NECESSARY TO
DISCOVER THE PROBLEM

Skillful counselors learn how to look beneath
and beyond what people say. They seek
hidden causes or misunderstandings that
the person being counseled may be
unable to sense because they are too
close to the problem. Counselors learn to
uncover these important aspects by
asking the right questions at the right time
and in the right manner.

EASY AS YOU GO!

SECOND BASE: IDENTIFY THE PROBLEM

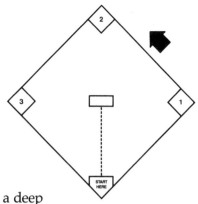

A problem needs to be seen clearly and understood before it can be solved. Your role as a counselor is to help others do this. The following suggestions should help.

Talking is therapeutic. People who want help usually have a deep need to talk things out. The more they do this in your presence the better. Be sure to provide them with sufficient time to get things out of their systems.

The blame game. Sometimes individuals need to blame others for predicaments before they understand that they themselves may be responsible. Give those you counsel time to do this. Do not become irritable during the process. It is often a hurdle that must be overcome before a person is ready to assume a different kind of behavior.

Problems are seen more clearly through verbalization. It is one thing to think things out in your head; it is something different to talk things out in front of another. Talking sometimes provides insights not possible through self-analysis. Keep reminding yourself that as a person talks she or he may be coming closer to an understanding of the problem.

Most problems involve relationships with others. Human conflicts are the most difficult to satisfactorily resolve. While listening to such a problem, it is important not to take sides. Although the individual you are working with may be partially at fault (there are usually two sides to any human conflict), it will take time for the person to sense it. Realization of the problem will often be recognized when alternatives to solve the conflict are studied.

**Things to Keep in Mind
When Going Toward Second Base**

1. Listen and be patient

2. Accept and don't judge

3. Question or restate for clarification

4. Remain objective

COUNSELING OBJECTIVITY

It is said that the closer someone is to you, the more difficult it becomes to advise that person. It is often more problematical for a mother to counsel her daughter than it would be to counsel someone else's daughter. The reason for this is because your emotions get tangled up in the counseling process. Generally speaking, the more objective the counselor, the better the results.

CASE 4

WILL GRAY GET TO SECOND BASE WITH HIS SON?

When it comes to his son, Tony, Gray has two primary goals. First, he wants to maintain a good father-son relationship. Second, he wants Tony to mature into a responsible adult. The situation is complicated because Gray and Diane, Tony's mother, divorced two years ago and Tony lives with his mother.

Last night Diane called and asked Gray to counsel their son on a series of problems including hostility toward school and his insistence that he is old enough to have his own car. Tony turned 16 two months ago.

Gray has arranged to spend Saturday afternoon with Tony. His plan is to take his son to a professional soccer game (Tony plays soccer in high school) and then sit in a quiet restaurant later to talk things over. His approach (once both are comfortable) is to say, ''Tony, your mother says things are not going too well for you right now. I thought we might talk about it.''

Once Tony starts talking, Gray hopes to accomplish the following.

1. Discover problems as Tony sees them.

2. Try to sense how the problems are interrelated.

3. Discover what Tony feels would solve the problems.

4. Find out *why* Tony thinks the solution (or solutions) would work.

If this is satisfactorily accomplished, Gray intends to delay his support of one solution over another until the following week. This will give him time to evaluate the options. It will also give him an opportunity to talk with his ex-wife. He feels strongly that both should be involved in whatever solution may be reached.

How does Gray plan to get to second base? Will his strategy get them there?__

Compare your answer to that of the authors on page 92.

MAKE THE MOVE
TO THIRD BASE

CHALLENGE AHEAD!

THE ELEGANT SOLUTION

For most problems, there are what professionals call elegant solutions. This is the **ideal** solution under the circumstances. It usually means that the person involved can live with the design and others will not be hurt beyond reason. Your job as a counselor is to help another to isolate the problem, fashion a solution and accept it as his or her own. This is a sensitive process that requires you to understand the feelings of the other party. It is not always easy for a person to accept a solution–even though it may be the best one under the circumstances.

56

THIRD BASE:
CLARIFY THE ALTERNATIVES

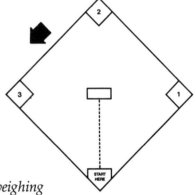

Counseling is the ability to help others through the decision-making process. Your role as an advisor is to help others *weigh and decide* which road to take. Academic counselors assist students in the selection of the right courses. Marriage counselors help individuals decide how to satisfactorily resolve marital problems. Supervisors help keep employees productive and positive.

Whatever your role, the counselor should emphasize the *weighing* part of the process, and let the other party do the *deciding*. Here are some suggestions.

Get several alternatives on the table. Frequently an advisor can suggest an alternative not previously considered by the person being counseled. In most situations, possibilities are greater than first perceived.

The weighing process is complex. To *weigh* means to compare and balance one possibility against all others. In a counseling situation this means plenty of discussion. Often the advisor must lead the party into the process and then record reactions of one alternative to another. Some minds are more capable of weighing than others. As a counselor, you need to mentally "try on" the alternatives so you can visualize what the outcomes might be with the different options.

Discarding alternatives. As a counselor, try to keep the party from throwing out possibilities prematurely. On the other hand, when a solution is obviously not close to being elegant, it should be discarded quickly. If you get alternatives down to the "Rule of Three" the efficiency of the process will improve. Weighing three possibilities is much easier than five or six.

Making the decision. If you listen and observe, you will get signals that suggest which solution is best for the party being counseled. These signals—plus your own understanding of the problem—can help direct the person counseled to the ideal solution. Still, the decision must be made by the other party, not you. Do not rush the process. In many cases you will find yourself protecting the other party by asking him or her to carefully think it over.

VOICE CONTROL

Effective counselors, like actors and actresses, quickly learn to appreciate the importance of their voices. An agitated, loud voice is upsetting to the person being helped. A quiet, modulated voice contributes measurably to the right counseling atmosphere. It is an excellent idea for anyone preparing to improve his or her counseling techniques to tape record and listen carefully to the tone of that voice. Even better, "mock" counseling sessions with a friend (going around the four bases of a problem), followed by a critique, can improve self-confidence and build a better counseling style. This kind of practice is highly recommended.

CASE 5

LETTING THE CLIENT MAKE THE CHOICE

Reverend Stacy received a call from John and Mary Jones yesterday requesting a counseling appointment. One was arranged for this afternoon. Both John and Mary have been active congregation members for over twenty years. They have never asked for counseling before.

The approach was easy but the anxiety on Mary's face was obvious. John seemed depressed. Getting them to talk openly about the problem took time but it eventually came out. John has had a deepening conflict with his superior at work and has been threatened with dismissal. His boss was recently promoted to president of the company, and now has even more control over John's future. Reverend Stacy knew how serious the conflict was when John admitted he had been on sedatives for several months. After an hour of discussion, Reverend Stacy made the move to third base by saying: "Let's list the alternatives to this unfortunate situation."

Through discussion, the following possibilities were listed:

- Try to hang in for three years in order to take an early retirement
- Seek a transfer within the corporation, so he would not have to report to the president
- Accept a lower position with less pressure
- Retire now
- Resign and make a career change
- Initiate an age-discrimination suit (John is 59)

A confrontation with John's superior was ruled out because John tried this on one occasion and all that happened was a more intense, hate-filled relationship. The conflict seems to be irreconcilable.

After a discussion of each alternative, it was decided to narrow choices to the three year "sweat it out" period, seek a transfer, or retire now. John cannot bring himself to accept a lower position and he is not up to a career change. An age discrimination suit would add more stress and push John into deeper psychological turmoil. Noticing, at this point, that both John and Mary seem pleased with the progress but fatigued beyond the point of being able to make a sound decision, Reverend Stacy suggests that all three study and evaluate the remaining alternatives and meet again the following afternoon.

How would you rate Reverend Stacy as a counselor?

Excellent ☐ Good ☐ Weak ☐

Compare your rating with that of the author on page 92.

END OF COUNSELING SESSION GOALS

You will know you are approaching home base when the following occurs:

- The person you are helping can see the light (solution) at the end of the tunnel.

- The individual has developed the necessary confidence to select the best available alternative and make a decision.

- The person's burden has been (at least partially) lifted. Self-esteem has been restored.

GETTING HOME SAFELY

HOME BASE: CLOSING THE SESSION

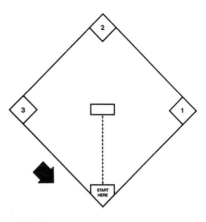

It is usually up to the counselor to terminate the counseling. This process starts on third base where (hopefully) alternatives have been isolated. As you help the person you are counseling select the elegant solution, consider weaving the following steps into your style:

Ask the individual to restate and review the decision. This is important because it ensures that an agreement has been reached. If necessary, the counselor may wish to articulate the implications of the decision. **(Skill: ask/listen/accept)**

Help to reinforce the individual's self-esteem. Whether a decision has been reached or not (sometimes it takes additional sessions), it is important that the party leaves feeling better. Counseling should be an uplifting experience for both parties. Always compliment the person being counseled toward the end of the session. State that you are encouraged with the progress.
(Skill: be optimistic/supportive)

Discuss how the solution is to be implemented. In most situations, the counselor can make suggestions about how the person can proceed in the future. These are often little things that can be said easily. The session has produced the right road to take, now it is permissible to provide certain warnings about possible detours, sharp turns, etc.
(Skill: promote confidence in decisions)

How does the decision relate to the individual's goal? Will it make the goal easier to reach? Does it reinforce the existing goal? Is a stronger goal needed?

Leave the door open for a return visit. Counselors more often than not build lasting relationships with those they assist. This makes it easy for the individual to return voluntarily. Even so, an invitation to return is reinforcing. An experienced counselor knows that a single counseling session seldom solves a major problem. A return visit to you, the counselor, is a compliment. **(Skill: accept/support)**

ADVANCE PLANNING

In certain situations, a counselor knows in advance that a difficult session is inevitable. Trouble is on the horizon. Under these conditions it is possible, and sometimes advisable, for the counselor to devise a game plan in advance. The danger in doing this is a loss of flexibility. The counselor might try so hard to make the game plan work that he or she does not listen to the other party, and the actual problem never gets identified or resolved. It may be advisable to go into a session with a plan; but once communication starts, it is usually better to play things by ear. Counselors with preconceived ideas are often their own worst enemies.

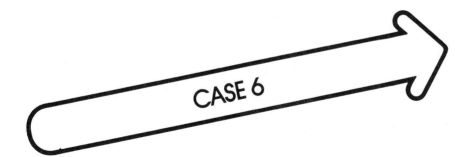

CASE 6

COUNSELING STRATEGY

No question about it, Wayne is the best quarterback Valley High has had in a decade. But the publicity has apparently inflated his ego. As a result, Wayne is no longer a good team player: He is frequently late to practice and resentment against Wayne among team players is growing.

With league playoffs just two weeks away (Valley High has already qualified), Coach Jennings is disturbed. Without Wayne their chances are poor. However, unless Wayne changes his attitude, the rest of the team may not perform to its potential. After thinking it over, the coach decides on a strategy.

Tomorrow, after practice, he will ask Wayne to come by his office. Using a nondirective approach, Coach Jennings hopes to get an open conversation started where he can point out to Wayne that college scouts will be present during the playoffs and that Wayne needs the support of the entire team to look his best. He plans to cover all the bases with Wayne, hoping he will get the picture without having to spell things out.

After this session, if Wayne doesn't get rid of his cocky attitude, Coach Jennings will use a directive approach. He will get tough and lay it on the line with Wayne. He will communicate that he will not stand for Wayne's behavior and will demand a positive change or bench Wayne.

How Does Coach Jennings' Counseling Strategy Include the Skills and Principles That You Learned in This Program?

Check those that he used:

The Five Rs:
☐ Why? The Right Purpose ☐ When? The Right Time
☐ Where? The Right Place ☐ What? The Right Approach
☐ How? The Right Technique

The Four Bases:
☐ Listen—First Base ☐ Clarify Alternatives—Third Base
☐ Identify the Problem—Second Base ☐ Choose and Accept a Solution—Home Base

The Basic Counseling Skills:
☐ Learn ☐ Accept ☐ Listen ☐ Confirm ☐ Be Optimistic
☐ Objectivity ☐ Confidential ☐ Promote Decision Making ☐ Offer Support

Compare your views with those of the authors on page 92.

LEARNING FROM EXPERIENCE

Counseling isn't something one can learn quickly. Like scuba diving or other demanding sports, the more preparation the better, and experience is necessary to reach high levels of competency. Everytime you counsel you should learn something. Always try to adjust your behavior to accommodate what you have learned so you won't have to relearn it the next time.

AFTER EACH EXPERIENCE, RATE YOURSELF ON HOW TO MAKE IMPROVEMENTS THE NEXT TIME AROUND.

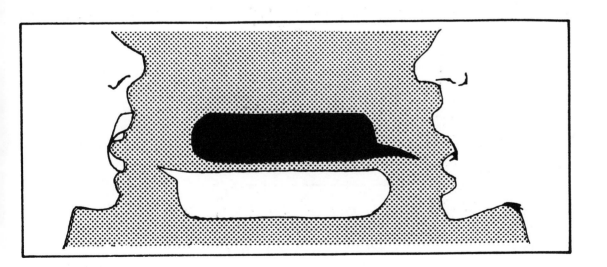

GO AROUND THE BASES ONCE MORE —IN REVIEW

In the months ahead, keep the comparison between baseball and counseling in mind. Make a serious attempt to cover all four bases in each session. To help you remember to do this, please write out (in your own words) what you hope to accomplish at each base. Do this now.

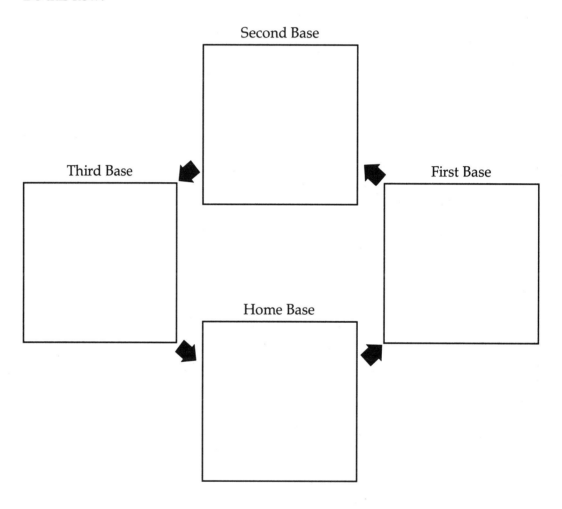

On the following pages you will find two hypothetical counseling scenarios that may help you in sensing just how a supervisor (counselor) might take an employee (counselee) around the four bases. You are encouraged to read each scenario and answer the questions provided.

HYPOTHETICAL COUNSELING SCENARIO #1
(Phillip takes Brent around the four bases)

First Base: Phillip has been concerned for weeks about Brent's productivity gap. Brent, in comparison to previous months, has seemed listless and unwilling to work anywhere near his true potential. During a routine coffee break, Phillip (Brent's supervisor) asks, ''Brent, I get the feeling you have temporarily lost your enthusiasm around here. If I am wrong, please forgive my intruding. If I am right, is there anything I can do about it?'' Phillip listens while Brent admits his lack of motivation and talks for five minutes about certain problems.

Second Base: "What do you think is the underlying problem, Brent?" asks Phillip. "Is the problem work-oriented?" Brent replies, "It's hard for me to know. Perhaps it is because I just don't see a future for me around here, or at least a future bright enough." Phillip asks, "Could it be that you have lost sight of your previous goals? Your personal productivity was high your first year." "Yeah, I guess that is it," Brent says. The two of them discuss Brent's previous goals and over a period of twenty minutes decide they are good goals and should be sufficiently powerful to motivate Brent.

Third Base: "May I offer a possible solution?" asks Phillip. "Sure," replies Brent. "Well," starts Phillip, "it seems we are on the wrong track. You have good goals, but we expect them to motivate you automatically. I don't think it works that way. I think you expect someone else to motivate you in the direction of your goals, when this is your job. Self-motivation is the name of the game these days. All I can do is provide the best possible working environment. The motivation must come from inside you. Am I right?" Brent starts talking about how he seems to get his productivity up for a few days and then it all fades away. He states that he does not seem able to find himself. Brent discusses this and related thoughts for ten minutes.

Home Base: Phillip knows they have reached home base when Brent says, ''You know, I'm glad we had this talk. I think it has caused me to refocus on my goals, and if you feel that my co-workers are providing their own motivation, then I am willing to see if I can do the same. Give me thirty days and let's review what has happened.''

Please answer the following questions:

Is the scenario realistic?	YES ☐ NO ☐
Were all four bases covered?	YES ☐ NO ☐
Does this hypothetical case provide you with a four-base pattern that might help you develop one of your own?	YES ☐ NO ☐
Did the meeting help Brent isolate his *real* problem?	YES ☐ NO ☐
Will Brent be able to motivate himself on a more permanent basis?	YES ☐ NO ☐

HYPOTHETICAL COUNSELING SCENARIO #2
(Alice takes Jane around the four bases)

First Base: It is midafternoon and supervisor Alice has invited employee Jane into her private office. She asks the receptionist to hold all telephone calls. When Jane is comfortably seated and they have talked briefly about Jane's new hairstyle, Alice says: "I've been meaning to ask you for some time how things are going for you and what success you are having in balancing home and career." Jane starts out by saying that she is finding it increasingly difficult because one of her two children is frequently ill and other problems keep surfacing. It takes ten minutes to cover first base.

Second Base: "It is tough to raise two children alone and hold down a demanding job but there must be a few things we can consider that will help. Can we make a list?" Alice asks. Jane agrees and during the next ten minutes they isolate the following problems.

Children frequently ill

Weekend planning insufficient

Too much time devoted to shopping

Not enough sleep

Too much social activity

Car problems

Children's day care arrangements

Third Base: "With our list in mind," asks Alice, "what can be done to reduce some or all of the problems to size?" A conversation around this question lasts for five minutes when Jane says: "I think the basic problem is that I cannot seem to organize myself." "I think you have something there," replied Alice, "I really do. If we put our heads together, I think we can help you become an organized person. If so, both your home and work hours will improve. Want to try?" "Yes," replies Jane, "and the sooner the better. To be honest with you, I knew why you called me in this afternoon. I know that I have not been producing at a high enough level. Besides, my co-workers are tired of my being late and absent so often. I want to be better organized so things will work out better. I really do."

Home Base: The next twenty minutes were spent working out a step-by-step plan that would help Jane become a better-organized single parent. A few of the steps were: (1) Jane would write out a task priority list for each day. (2) On Sunday before going shopping, she would prepare a menu for the children and herself for each day of the week. (3) She would develop a reward system to encourage both children to be more disciplined and *not* call mother at work. (4) She would follow a more definite maintenance schedule on her car.

When the plan was complete Jane said to Alice, ''Thanks for your help. I hope you will be pleased with results.''

Please answer the following questions:

Does this scenario help you understand the four-step baseball analogy better?　　YES ☐ NO ☐

Did Alice do right by not telling Jane the reason for their counseling session?　　YES ☐ NO ☐

Were all four bases covered in a satisfactory manner?　　YES ☐ NO ☐

Do you think this session will help Jane solve her problems?　　YES ☐ NO ☐

Did the meeting improve the relationship between Alice and Jane?　　YES ☐ NO ☐

> "In those days he was wiser than he is now
> —he used to frequently take my advice."
>
> Winston Churchill

IV

Counseling With Enthusiasm And Style

PROFESSIONAL STANDARDS

Almost every aspect of life has certain standards of behavior. Teachers, supervisors, nurses, law officers and others have ethical practices to which they try to conform. Anyone who counsels or advises others should conform to accepted practices of honesty, integrity and good human relations skills.

DANGERS AHEAD

SIX UNFORGIVABLE MISTAKES

☐ **Overtalking and underlistening.** You may never learn the real problem.

☐ **Acting like a psychologist or clinical counselor when you are not.** The individual might expect therapy, which you are not qualified to deliver.

☐ **Prying into the personal life of the individual you are attempting to help.** It might destroy the counseling relationship.

☐ **Using a counseling relationship to your own advantage.** This violates your primary role as a helper.

☐ **Failure to keep information obtained from a counseling relationship confidential.** Otherwise you will be labeled as a person who cannot be trusted.

☐ **Making decisions for the person being counseled.** They won't learn how to make quality decisions. Also, if things don't work out, they can blame you.

> **YOU NEED NOT HAVE HAD FORMAL TRAINING TO BE A GOOD COUNSELOR. HOWEVER, DON'T CONFUSE YOUR ROLE WITH PROFESSIONAL CLINICAL COUNSELING. SOME PROBLEMS CAN BE HANDLED ONLY BY EXPERTS.**

COUNSELING STYLE AND PERSONALITY

With practice, you will develop your own counseling style based on your personality. You need not change your personality to become an effective counselor. You should recognize, however, that different people react differently to the same personality. This means that not all of the people you counsel will react to you in the same way. You may need to give some more time to adjust to you. A few may not adjust well at all. **This should be anticipated.** All counselors, no matter how skilled, can have unsuccessful experiences.

The thing to remember is to do your best and learn as you gain experience. Be proud of your counseling style and be proud of yourself!

To become an excellent counselor, you must **expect** to become one.

COUNSELING STYLE QUIZ

Below are 10 true or false statements. Place a T or F in each square and compare your answers with those at the bottom of the page.

☐ 1. A counselor who is under pressure to complete a session by a certain time is severely handicapped.

☐ 2. Any sexual overtones that develop during a counseling session are distracting and unprofessional.

☐ 3. Counselors are trained to give advice.

☐ 4. Counselors should frequently evaluate themselves to make certain they have not developed irritating habits.

☐ 5. Most people enter into an "intervention" counseling session with some degree of apprehension.

☐ 6. Counselors should quickly terminate a session once the problem has been identified.

☐ 7. In a counseling session, your attitude can speak so loudly the other party cannot hear what you say.

☐ 8. Counseling others should be considered an opportunity and not a job.

☐ 9. The individual being counseled should never be made to feel embarrassed, immature or guilty.

☐ 10. Only professionals should counsel.

ANSWERS: 1. T (It may not be the right time and it may be difficult to listen.) 2. T (That could distract from the real purpose and may make objectivity difficult. It also could lead to a law suit!) 3. F (They are trained to listen and promote decision making.) 4. T (Failure to establish rapport may prevent an otherwise capable counselor from getting to first base.) 5. T (And this makes optimism on your part very important.) 6. F (You are only on second base and you must get to third and home before you score.) 7. T (No matter how good your ideas, the client must "hear" to act.) 8. T (It should be mutually rewarding.) 9. T (Listen and accept; don't judge and reject.) 10. F (Counseling skills can be used by all of us in our daily lives.)

TOTAL CORRECT: ☐

PRACTICE DOESN'T ALWAYS MAKE PERFECT

As is true in other repetitive situations, many people who play golf on a regular schedule can fall into bad habits. That is why it is possible for someone who has never played golf to take lessons and, by following the right techniques, do as well as or better than someone who has played for years.

The same is true with personal counseling. Even if you have never had any experience or training in the counseling process, you can do extremely well in a relatively short period of time by *following the rules.* You might discover you can do as well as or better than those with considerable experience who have become careless about the basics.

Counseling is a skill that you can learn and adapt to your own personality. With patience and practice you will, as in golf, be pleased with your score.

CASE #7

DISCOVERING WEAKNESSES

Over the years, Anthony has developed the reputation as a good person to take a problem to. As a manager with over 20 employees under his supervision, he spends more time counseling than others in a similar position. Anthony even has workers from other departments come to him for advice. Around home, neighbors frequently seek his guidance.

Anthony's wife has this to say: "My husband is a natural counselor. He is patient, concerned and an outstanding listener. Somehow people understand their own problems better after talking with him. Even our own kids take some of their problems to their father. Strange as it may seem, he has never read a book or taken a course in counseling."

Obviously, Anthony has some natural counseling skills that he has improved upon through experience over the years. He seems to do things right without knowing why. Under this situation, do you think that knowing the Five Rs of counseling would make him even more effective? Would understanding the baseball analogy help Anthony improve his skills and enhance his already positive reputation as a counselor? Please provide answers to the following questions and compare them to those of the Authors on page 92.

The Five Rs of counseling could help (or hurt) Anthony's counseling effectiveness for the following reasons:

_____

_____

_____

The baseball analogy could help (or hurt) Anthony's effectiveness as a counselor for the following reasons:

_____

_____

_____

As skillful as Anthony appears to be, learning more about the counseling process could help him discover weaknesses in his style.

Yes ☐   No ☐

WIN-WIN RELATIONSHIPS

There are times when an open discussion between two people can make both parties winners. In such cases, neither person is a counselor; but if sound counseling techniques are used the discussion will probably be productive.

The long-term success of any human relationship is dependent upon both people coming out ahead. For this to happen, there must be somewhat of a balance between the rewards each individual receives from the other. When one party winds up doing too much giving, the relationship usually deteriorates. The philosophy of an equal reward system is the basis of the Mutual Reward Theory (MRT).

When two people can sit down and openly discuss the rewards they can provide each other, the relationship should measurably improve. Both parties should come out ahead.

RESOLVE CONFLICTS USING MRT

MRT AS A SOLUTION TO HUMAN CONFLICTS

The Mutual Reward Theory (MRT) is based upon a system of somewhat equal rewards between two people. When this occurs, both individuals come out ahead and the relationship between them becomes stronger. Although MRT can be used to build new relationships and strengthen old ones, its best use is to repair or restore impaired relationships. Sometimes, as a counselor, you may have the opportunity to suggest that a counselee might use MRT to solve a relationship conflict. By teaching the MRT idea, you would be giving the counselee a tool they could use to solve their own conflict. In effect, you would be helping the counselee solve her or his problem.

Assume that those in the abbreviated cases that follow are your counselees. Place a check mark opposite those that you feel could make use of MRT.

☐ 1. Mark's attitude at work has drastically deteriorated. Where once he was a candidate for promotion, his supervisor would now like to see him resign. The supervisor feels it may be too late to save Mark for the organization.

☐ 2. Marsha and her 17-year-old daughter love each other dearly but are constantly fighting over trivial matters. Marsha senses the close relationship they once knew may be gone forever.

☐ 3. Dr. Henry, advisor to the high school student council, is at odds with Drake, the student body president. Drake keeps advocating items he knows will irritate Dr. Henry. As a result, council meetings are a disaster and the quality of student activities on campus is far below previous standards.

☐ 4. Susanne has reached the breaking point. For the past year she has held down a demanding job as well as doing 95 percent of the work around the apartment. Charles pays 50 percent of expenses, but that's it. Susanne would like to restore a good relationship but sees little hope.

☐ 5. Maria feels the relationship with her father is all give on her part and no understanding on his. Although she would prefer to stay home with her mother and sisters, now that she is 18 and has a good full-time job she is tempted to leave.

> The authors feel MRT counseling is appropriate in all five situations. The MRT goals could be: (1) Mark's attitude toward the job improves and the supervisor's attitude toward Mark improves. (2) Neither party wants to fight: both could come out ahead by pulling back. (3) Both are unhappy and the goals of the council are suffering. A reversal *could* take place. (4) If both parties discuss the situation and agree to more equally divide the tasks, the situation should improve. (5) As the relationship with her father improves, Maria could feel closer to the rest of the family; the two younger sisters would benefit.

MANY SUPERVISORS AND TEACHERS AVOID
COUNSELING MEETINGS WITH THOSE FROM
FOREIGN CULTURES BECAUSE THEY FEAR
COMMUNICATION PROBLEMS THAT CAN
RESULT IN MISUNDERSTANDINGS. THIS IS
UNFORTUNATE BECAUSE THOSE FROM
OTHER CULTURES ALSO HAVE PROBLEMS
THAT REQUIRE GUIDANCE.

SOLUTION?

ACCEPT SUCH MEETINGS AS A CHALLENGE
WHERE YOU CAN LEARN AS MUCH AS THE
COUNSELEE.

COUNSELING PEOPLE FROM OTHER CULTURES

Whether you are a teacher, supervisor, youth leader or clergyman, the person opposite you in a communications session of the future may have difficulty with the English language and/or understanding our culture. In simple terms, this means the communications bridge is more difficult to cross. How should you, as a personal counselor, deal with this possibility? Here are some suggestions.

► **Slow down the counseling process.** Use the same principles and techniques that you use with those fluent in English and already fully adjusted to our culture, but be satisfied to move at a more leisurely pace. Perhaps schedule two or three sessions instead of one.

► **Encourage the use of English.** Most immigrants can speak more English than they at first demonstrate because they fear they might say the wrong thing. Give them the confidence to speak up as much as possible and compliment them when they do.

► **Inject more laughter.** To give yourself more patience and help the individual relax, laugh at your attempts to understand each other. If you know a few words in their language, use them.

► **Use illustrations.** Often it is possible to sketch what you are trying to say through symbols. For example, you can explain the counseling process by sketching and explaining the baseball analogy.

► **Wait longer for answers.** It will be natural for the individual from a foreign culture to take more time in answering a question or asking one. Give them the time to struggle without restating the question.

► **Explain our jargon and idioms.** When you see a blank stare in their eyes, smile and do your best to explain through gestures what your odd expression really means.

► **Be generous in giving compliments.** Use hand gestures, your smile of approval and the laughter of your eyes to indicate progress—no matter how slowly the process is moving.

► **If a translator is avilable, call for help!** Communicating through an interpreter can and should be a lively and enjoyable treat for any counselor. If circumstances permit, do not pass up this opportunity.

Don't be tempted to give advice or make decisions for the counselee. It is very common in most other cultures to look to authority figures (you) for the ''right'' advice.

WINDING UP THE PROCESS

IN PERSONAL COUNSELING, AFTER A
PROBLEM HAS BEEN DISCUSSED, OPTIONS
CLARIFIED AND A DECISION MADE, IT IS
IMPORTANT THAT COUNSELEES LEAVE WITH
A POSITIVE ATTITUDE TOWARD THEMSELVES
AND THEIR FUTURES.

THE COUNSELING PROCESS HAS NOT BEEN
COMPLETED UNTIL THIS HAPPENS.

SOMETIMES AN APPROPRIATE COMPLIMENT
WILL DO THE TRICK.

MENTORING

Mentoring can be defined as one person, usually senior in age
and status, having a significant and beneficial effect on the life
of the other. Recognized mentors are usually skillful at personal
counseling. For additional information on mentoring and how it
relates to personal counseling the publication *Mentoring: A
Practical Guide* by Gordon F. Shea is recommended. To order
this or other FIFTY MINUTE™ self-study publications, use the
information in the back of this book.

INSTILLING CONFIDENCE

When you view counseling as a communications opportunity to help another person solve a problem (or problems) you suddenly realize that the most important thing you can do is to give the individual the confidence to move ahead and implement the solution. How do you instill this confidence?

Often it means reinforcement through sincere and deserved compliments. Assume, for a moment, that you have devoted an hour or so counseling an individual and you are pleased with the results. Toward the end of the session, you might give one or more of the following compliments. Please check, in the boxes provided, the three you would be most apt to use.

☐ Compliment the person on arriving at his or her decision.

☐ State that from your point of view the solution appears reasonable and reachable.

☐ Say, ''Everyone needs a challenge. You have given yourself one and you can achieve it.''

☐ Suggest that having made this decision, the person is better prepared to make others.

☐ Say, ''I have noticed an increase in your confidence during the time we have spent together.''

☐ Say, ''It seems to me you look better and act better to others than you think you do.''

☐ State that things work out for people who try.

☐ Say, ''You've got the right stuff. All you need is the confidence to use it.''

Viewed from a distance, a counseling experience can be an exercise in goal setting for the person being counseled.

When an individual walks away from a successful counseling experience, she or he should have (1) reaffirmed a previous goal or (2) established a new one.

REVIEW

RATE YOUR COUNSELING SKILLS

As you progress toward becoming an effective, successful counselor, it is a good idea to rate yourself after each session. This form is designed for this purpose. If you rate yourself as a 5 in any category, you are saying that further improvement is not possible; if you rate yourself a 3 or below, you are saying improvement is necessary.

		High				Low
1.	**Approach:** A nonthreatening climate was created. Both parties were relaxed and communicated easily. (Right approach)	5	4	3	2	1
2.	**Talking:** The person being counseled did most of the talking and opened up easily. (First base)	5	4	3	2	1
3.	**Listening:** Because I worked to hear what was said, it was possible to identify the problem easily. (Second base)	5	4	3	2	1
4.	**Voice:** I modulated my voice. It was soft, nonirritating and communicated warmth. (Accepting)	5	4	3	2	1
5.	**Identification of problem:** Both parties agreed the true, underlying problem had been uncovered. (Second base/objectivity)	5	4	3	2	1
6.	**Solving problems:** We listed and discussed several alternatives and came up with an elegant solution. (Third base/home base)	5	4	3	2	1
7.	**Questions:** I did my best to ask the right questions at the right time. (Right time/when)	5	4	3	2	1
8.	**Terminating interview:** The session ended in an upbeat manner. The door was left open for the party to return. (Optimistic)	5	4	3	2	1
9.	**Empathy:** Both parties had feelings of understanding for each other. (Rapport)	5	4	3	2	1
10.	**Sensitivity:** I was sensitive to the needs, feelings and behavior of the person being counseled. The individual left the session feeling good. (Supportive)	5	4	3	2	1

MAKE THIS
YOUR PERSONAL
SUCCESS FORMULA

SOME FAIL TO BECOME EFFECTIVE
COUNSELORS BECAUSE THEY FORGET THE
FUNDAMENTALS. THE FORMULA ON THE NEXT
PAGE WILL ACT AS A REMINDER TO HELP YOU
SUCCEED AND BECOME INCREASINGLY
PROFESSIONAL IN THE DAYS AHEAD.

COUNSELING SUCCESS FORMULA

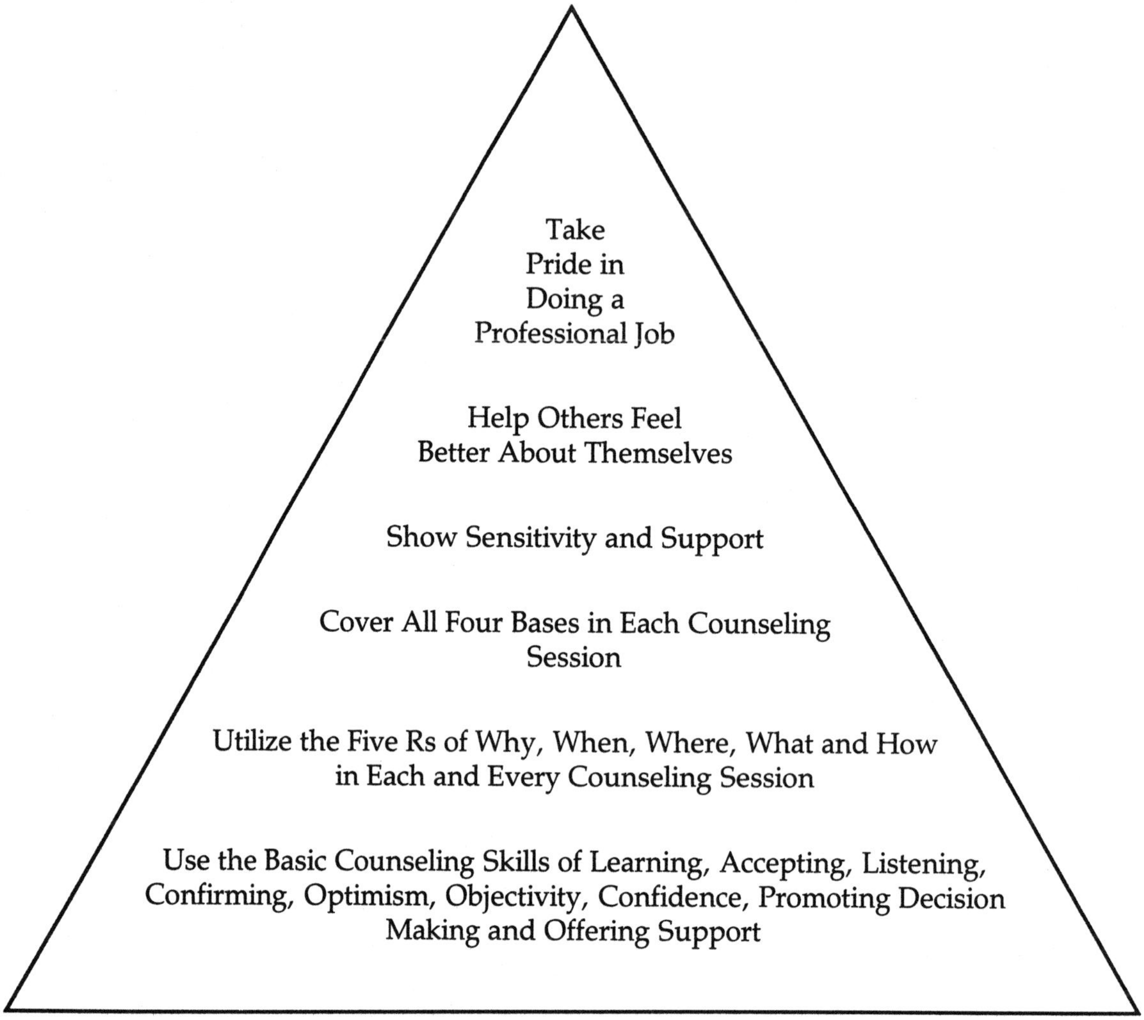

Take
Pride in
Doing a
Professional Job

Help Others Feel
Better About Themselves

Show Sensitivity and Support

Cover All Four Bases in Each Counseling
Session

Utilize the Five Rs of Why, When, Where, What and How
in Each and Every Counseling Session

Use the Basic Counseling Skills of Learning, Accepting, Listening,
Confirming, Optimism, Objectivity, Confidence, Promoting Decision
Making and Offering Support

IT IS NOW TIME TO MEASURE THE
PROGRESS YOU HAVE MADE.
ON THE FOLLOWING PAGE ARE 20
STATEMENTS THAT ARE EITHER TRUE
OR FALSE. EACH IS WORTH FIVE
POINTS. ANSWERS WILL BE FOUND
ON PAGE 91.

SCORE YOURSELF

DEMONSTRATE YOUR PROGRESS

For each statement below, put a check mark under true or false.

True   False

1. Counseling is primarily problem solving.
2. Selecting the *right* person is one of the 5 Rs of counseling.
3. Becoming a good counselor should measurably improve your career progress.
4. Few people have the right stuff to become good counselors.
5. The less talking you do as a counselor the more effective you will be.
6. Intervention counseling is very difficult.
7. Only highly trained professionals should counsel.
8. A good counselor is one who helps others find elegant solutions to their problems.
9. The job of the counselor is to weigh alternatives and let the person being counseled make the decision.
10. MRT works best when an individual needs to maintain a healthy relationship with the other party.
11. Sometimes individuals need to blame others before they admit they are responsible.
12. Acting like a psychologist or clinical counselor is not one of the unforgivable mistakes.
13. To become a good counselor one must go through a personality change.
14. Quiet people seldom become successful counselors.
15. The best place to identify a person's problem is on home base.
16. No matter how a session turns out, a skillful counselor always makes the other party feel better.
17. Without a positive attitude, becoming a good counselor is impossible.
18. Most counselors fail because of insensitive behavior.
19. The way to become a professional counselor is to analyze mistakes after each session and then make behavioral changes so the mistakes are not repeated.
20. It is difficult to get around the bases if you are uncomfortable with your counselor.

TOTAL   Turn page for answers.

1. T — In order to work, you must get around all four bases.

2. F — The person is **a given**. The five Rs are why and how you go about counseling.

3. T — Counseling skills are basic to success in many roles, especially that of a supervisor or manager.

4. F — It simply takes a desire to help people, along with good skills.

5. T — The most important counseling skill is **listening**; the least important is **giving advice**.

6. T — This is usually true because the behavior of the person to be counseled has caused a problem.

7. F — Most intelligent adults can develop the skills to help people solve problems.

8. T — Too often counselors are advice-givers rather than solution-seekers.

9. T — The person should make his or her own decision.

10. T — MRT works best in a relationship where both continue to benefit.

11. T — A good counselor can help an individual get beyond this stage.

12. F — You must be realistic about what you are qualified to do.

13. F — You've got the right stuff the way you are.

14. F — Quiet people become excellent counselors.

15. F — It is second base.

16. T — A major counseling task is to promote self-esteem.

17. T — Your attitude is always communicated.

18. T — Talking too much, for instance, can lead to failure.

19. T — Constant review is essential.

20. T — Rapport between counselor and counselee is essential.

AUTHORS' SUGGESTED ANSWERS TO CASES

Page 12. Who will make the best counselor? Although both Byron and Ginger could become outstanding counselors, the authors feel Ginger may have a better chance because she will not permit her ambitions to get in the way. Byron appears to be so ambitious and ego-centered that he may have trouble relaxing to the point where he could do a sensitive job of counseling. He might lose patience and attempt to impose his solutions on others.

Page 20. What constitutes an excellent counselor? The authors believe that the most helpful characteristics found in each individual are: Geraldine: As an organized person, she is most apt to learn and follow a proven pattern. Jack: As a people person, he should be able to quickly build a rapport with each counselee. Genevieve: Her enjoyable personality should help counselees to relax. Each individual, however, may have a disadvantage. Geraldine may be too structured, Jack may never get around to helping the counselees solve problems, and Genevieve may enjoy the process so much the problem to be solved is not taken as seriously as it should be. When you add it all up, each person may have close to the same potential for success.

Page 40. Which approach is best? All three approaches could conceivably work (depending upon Justine's skills as a counselor) but the authors prefer approach #3 because it is more problem-centered than the others. Sally's on-the-job future depends upon her ability to balance her home and career. This is a difficult problem and alternatives need to be explored. Approach #3 leads quickly into the counseling process.

Page 54. Will Gray get to second base with his son? Gray is in a tight spot. His strategy and techniques to get to second base appear excellent, but success may depend more upon his past relationship than anything else. The most difficult person to counsel is often the person closest to you. Talking over what he feels to be the best solution with his ex-wife is vital to avoid Tony playing one parent against the other.

Page 58. Letting the client make the choice. The authors rate Reverend Stacy as an excellent counselor. He appears to have the skill of guiding others toward an elegant solution and then backing away from making it himself. In this instance, he provides additional time to discuss alternatives. Chances are good that Mr. and Mrs. Jones will come up with the best solution and live with it gracefully.

Page 62. Counseling strategy. Coach Jennings seems to be coming up with too little too late. It is difficult to understand why he has not counseled Wayne on the problem as it developed. Perhaps the coach lacks confidence in his counseling skills. Wayne *needs* guidance and would probably accept it if done with sensitivity. Problems seldom solve themselves. Coach Jennings' ''game plan'' to bench Wayne if he doesn't do a turnaround within a week could cause the coach to be overthreatening. More flexibility is recommended.

Page 78. Discovering weaknesses. It is possible that Anthony may be ignoring one or more of the Five Rs and, as a result, he is less effective than he would otherwise be. Following the baseball pattern could help get Anthony to the solution to the counselees problem faster. In fact, we do not have any evidence in the case that he is actually solving problems. He may be satisfying his own ego instead of helping the individual being counseled search for and find a solution. In finding weaknesses, Anthony could make changes and become more professional without losing the magic touch he seems to have with people.

APPLICATION OF YOUR NEW
COUNSELING SKILLS

The sooner you apply what you have learned the better. It is recommended that you set up two or three counseling situations as soon as it is practical. Before you enter into each session, make preparations by reviewing this program. After you have finished each session, critique yourself by listing what you intend to do differently next time. **PRACTICE IS NECESSARY.** Continue until you are comfortable and fully satisfied with your role as a counselor.

APPLICATION OF COUNSELING SKILLS

Name of person with whom you will be working:

_____

ADVANCE PREPARATION:

     Purpose of session: _____

     Time scheduled: _____

     Place:_____

     Approach you intend to use: _____

     Techniques, general strategy: _____

     _____

POST CRITIQUE:

     SUCCESS ACHIEVED IN COVERING THE FOUR BASES:

     First base: _____

             _____

             _____

     Second base:_____

             _____

             _____

     Third base:_____

             _____

             _____

     Home base: _____

             _____

             _____

THINGS I WILL DO DIFFERENTLY NEXT TIME:

_____

_____

_____

_____

(This form may be copied)

NOTES

NOTES

OVER 150 BOOKS AND 35 VIDEOS AVAILABLE IN THE 50-MINUTE SERIES

We hope you enjoyed this book. If so, we have good news for you. This title is part of the best-selling *50-MINUTE™ Series* of books. All *Series* books are similar in size and identical in price. Many are supported with training videos.

To order *50-MINUTE* Books and Videos or request a free catalog, contact your local distributor or Crisp Publications, Inc., 1200 Hamilton Court, Menlo Park, CA 94025. Our toll-free number is (800) 442-7477.

50-Minute Series Books and Videos Subject Areas . . .

Management
Training
Human Resources
Customer Service and Sales Training
Communications
Small Business and Financial Planning
Creativity
Personal Development
Wellness
Adult Literacy and Learning
Career, Retirement and Life Planning

Other titles available from Crisp Publications in these categories

Crisp Computer Series
The Crisp Small Business & Entrepreneurship Series
Quick Read Series
Management
Personal Development
Retirement Planning